On a Mission for Good Nutrition!

Rebecca Sjonger

P9-ARA-974

Crabtree Publishing Company
www.crabtreebooks.com

Author
Rebecca Sjonger

Publishing plan research and development
Reagan Miller

Editors
Kathy Middleton
Reagan Miller

Proofreader
Crystal Sikkens

Consultant
Steve Sanders, Ed.D.,
Professor, Early Childhood Physical Activity,
University of South Florida

Design
Samara Parent

Photo research
Samara Parent

Production coordinator and prepress technician
Samara Parent

Print coordinator
Margaret Amy Salter

Photographs
Comstock: p. 15 (milk)
Ingram photo objects: p. 7 (orange, celery)
istockphoto: p. 8 (bottom), 15 (cottage cheese), 20 (raisins)
PhotoDisc 49: p. 7 (bread, cheese, strawberries),
 21 (raspberries, blueberries)
Thinkstock: p. 4, 12, 14, 16, 17 (top, bottom middle), 19
All other images by Shutterstock

Library and Archives Canada Cataloguing in Publication

Sjonger, Rebecca, author
    On a mission for good nutrition! / Rebecca Sjonger.

(Healthy habits for a lifetime)
Includes index.
Issued in print and electronic formats.
ISBN 978-0-7787-1880-2 (bound).--ISBN 978-0-7787-1884-0 (paperback).--
ISBN 978-1-4271-1625-3 (pdf).--ISBN 978-1-4271-1621-5 (html)

    1. Nutrition--Juvenile literature. 2. Children--Nutrition--Juvenile
literature. I. Title.

RA784.S6 2015   j613.2   C2015-903937-1
                                                   C2015-903938-X

Library of Congress Cataloging-in-Publication Data

Sjonger, Rebecca, author.
    On a mission for good nutrition! / Rebecca Sjonger.
       pages cm. -- (Healthy habits for a lifetime)
    Includes index.
    ISBN 978-0-7787-1880-2 (reinforced library binding) -- ISBN 978-0-7787-1884-0 (pbk.)
    -- ISBN 978-1-4271-1625-3 (electronic pdf) -- ISBN 978-1-4271-1621-5 (electronic html)
    1. Nutrition--Juvenile literature. 2. Diet--Juvenile literature. 3. Health--Juvenile
literature. I. Title.

TX355.S597 2016
613.2--dc23
                                            2015021740

Crabtree Publishing Company

Printed in Canada/102015/IH20150821

Published in Canada
Crabtree Publishing
616 Welland Ave.
St. Catharines, Ontario
L2M 5V6

Published in the United States
Crabtree Publishing
PMB 59051
350 Fifth Avenue, 59th Floor
New York, New York 10118

Published in the United Kingdom
Crabtree Publishing
Maritime House
Basin Road North, Hove
BN41 1WR

Published in Australia
Crabtree Publishing
3 Charles Street
Coburg North
VIC 3058

Contents

Healthy eating

There are many great reasons to eat foods that are healthy for you. The **nutrients** in them help your bones, muscles, skin, and teeth grow. They also give your body the **energy** it needs to be active throughout the day. Healthy eating helps you to focus and learn. It even helps you avoid getting sick!

Did you know that eating **nutritious** foods could help you live longer? Different foods help your body in different ways. That is why you need to eat a variety of foods.

Eating a variety of foods gives you the energy to move your body in different ways.

Healthy eating is just one important **habit**. You should also be active for at least 60 minutes each day. Then aim to sleep at least 10 hours every night.

The food groups

Aim to eat a mix of foods from different food groups, to be sure your body is getting all the nutrients it needs. Make sure you eat vegetables and fruits, **grains**, **proteins**, and **dairy** each day. Keep reading to learn more about each of these groups.

Foods that are not part of these groups are usually not nutritious. They may have sugar, salt, or solid fats added to them, which are not good for you.

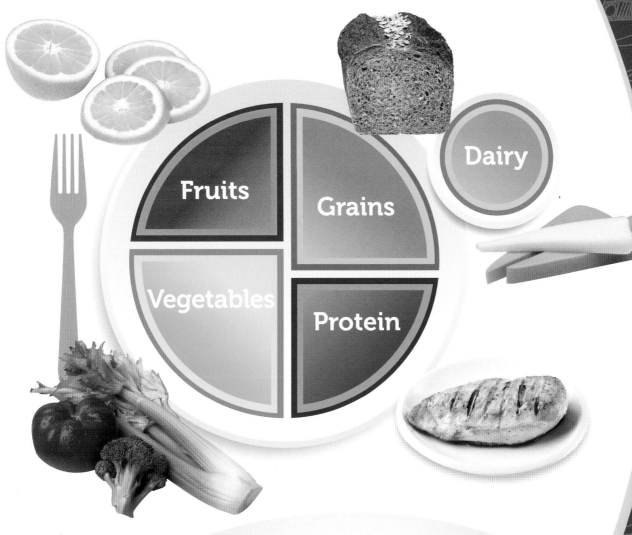

It is okay to have treats. Eat them in small amounts and not very often. Want a snack? Find something nutritious, such as berries or plain popcorn.

Vegetables and fruits

Vegetables and fruits are foods that come from plants. They are a great source of **minerals** and **vitamins**, which help your body work at its best. They boost your energy, too! There are different nutrients in different colored fruits and vegetables. For example, orange ones have a lot of vitamin C. Vitamin C helps your body heal if you are ill or wounded. Orange, red, and dark green foods that come from plants have the most nutrients. Try to eat the rainbow!

About half of what you eat should be vegetables and fruits. They can be fresh, dried, frozen, or canned. There are hundreds of different kinds of fruits! Have you ever tasted a dragon fruit? What about a horned melon? Ask your parents if you can choose a new fruit on your next shopping trip. You might find a new favorite!

Food is fresh if it looks like it does on the plant.

dragon fruit

horned melon

Your Daily Goal: Four or five **servings** of vegetables and fruits

Serving Suggestions: One medium-sized apple, one large carrot, or 20 grapes

9

Grains

Grains come from the dried seeds of grass-like plants. Many foods contain grains. You eat them when you have bread, cereal, crackers, pasta, or rice. Pizza crusts contain grains, too! One of the most important nutrients in grains is **fiber**. Its main role is to help waste move out of your body. Vegetables and fruits are also good sources of fiber.

Some foods are called "whole grain" because they contain all the parts of a seed. They have more nutrients than other grains. Oatmeal, whole-wheat pasta, and brown rice are examples of whole-grain foods.

Barley, rye, and wheat grains contain **gluten**. Eating this protein makes some people very sick and harms their bodies. They must eat gluten-free grains, such as corn, oats, and rice.

bagel

bread

pasta

Your Daily Goal: About four servings of grains
Serving Suggestions: Half of a small bagel, one slice of bread, or one-half cup (125 ml) of cooked pasta (about the size of a tennis ball).

Proteins

Proteins are nutrients that come from plants or animals. They build your bones and muscles. Proteins also help you to have healthy skin and blood. Plant-based foods that are high in protein include beans, nuts, and tofu. They also have fiber and healthy fats that your body needs to work properly.

Add proteins to each meal. Proteins, such as nuts, also make a great snack!

Protein also comes from animal-based foods, including eggs, meat, and seafood. Fish, such as wild salmon and sardines, are very high in protein. Lean meats contain less fat than other meats. They are a healthier choice of protein.

Go fish! Fish are a good source of lean protein. You can buy fish at the grocery store or catch them yourself!

Vegetarians are people who do not eat meat. They choose plant-based foods that have plenty of protein in them. Such as lentils, seeds, and nuts.

egg   *peanut butter*   *chicken*

Your Daily Goal: About two servings of proteins
Serving Suggestions: One egg, two tablespoons (30 ml) of peanut butter (about the size of a golf ball), or one-half cup (125 ml) of chicken (about the size of a tennis ball)

Dairy foods come from the milk of animals, such as cows and goats. Cheese, milk, and yogurt are common dairy products. They have minerals and vitamins that make your bones strong. The healthy fat in dairy foods helps kids' brains to develop.

Some people get sick from drinking or eating dairy products. They can use milk made from plants instead of dairy milk. Soy, almond, coconut, and rice milk are popular options.

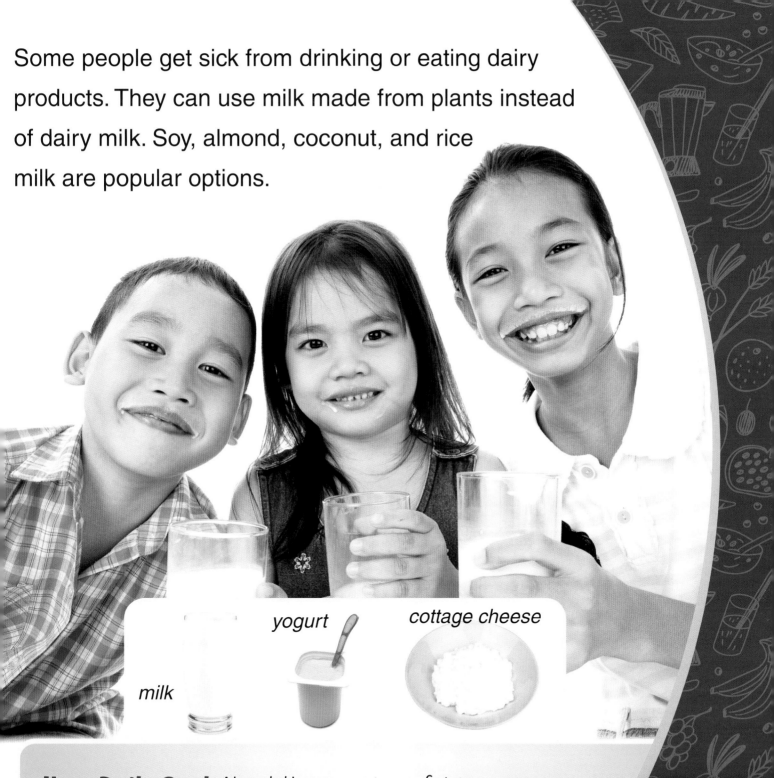

milk

yogurt

cottage cheese

Your Daily Goal: About three servings of dairy

Serving Suggestions: One cup (237 ml) of milk, yogurt, or cottage cheese—all about the size of a baseball

Water and oil

Your body needs water to survive. Thirst is your body's way of telling you that it is low on water. Make it a goal to drink water often so you do not get thirsty. Dairy and plant-based milks are also good to drink because they contain nutrients your body needs.

Many foods are also a source of water, including watermelon.

Juices are not as healthy as you think. They have a lot of sugar. Stick to small amounts of juices that have nothing added to them. Sodas are also loaded with sugar. They are not healthy for your body and should be avoided.

Water bottles that can be reused are good for the planet!

Oils are fats that become liquid when they are warm. Unlike solid fats, most oils have healthy nutrients. You should only eat them in small amounts, though. Oils are found in different food groups. For example, nuts, fish, and avocados all contain oil.

avocado

mayonnaise

mixed nuts

Your Daily Goal: About four tablespoons (60 ml) of healthy oils (about the size of two golf balls)

Serving Suggestions: Half of a medium-sized avocado, one tablespoon (15 ml) of mayonnaise (about the size of a thumb), or three tablespoons (44 ml) of mixed nuts (about three thumbs worth)

Tips for eating healthy

Read these healthy eating tips with a parent. What changes can your family make together?

Always have a healthy breakfast. Try to include all the food groups. Get as much ready as you can the night before. That way there will be less to do in the morning.

Can you help to plan and prepare meals at least one day a week? Cooking is a skill you can use your whole life!

Try a healthy snack instead of junk food. Maybe you will discover a new family favorite. Get started with the ideas on pages 20 and 21.

Do certain foods always make you feel ill? Be sure to tell your doctor about it!

Avoid eating at fast food restaurants. Instead, bring your own healthy meals and drinks when your family is on the go.

Make your own snack

Is all this talk about food making you hungry? Try making one of these healthy snack ideas!

Party Mix

Mix together about one cup (237 ml)—about the size of a baseball—of each of the following in a container:

- ▶ Whole-grain cereal
- ▶ Unsalted sunflower seeds
- ▶ Unsalted peanuts or your favorite kind of nuts
- ▶ Raisins or your favorite kind of dried fruits

Change up the amounts until you find a mix that is the perfect snack for you!

peanuts

sunflower seeds

raisins

measuring cup

whole-grain cereal

Frozen Fruit Pops

Try this cool snack on the next hot day:

1. Gather some toothpicks and rinse blueberries, raspberries, or grapes.
2. Stick a toothpick into each piece of fruit.
3. You can also stack two different fruits on one toothpick.
4. Place your fruit on a plate and put it in the freezer.
5. Wait one hour and then enjoy your frozen fruit!
6. Next time try using different fruits.

raspberries

blueberries

grapes

toothpicks

Show what you know!

Jared needs your help to pack a nutritious lunch. Which foods do you think are the healthiest choices?

Choose a drink:

water

sports drink

drinking box

Choose a protein:

chicken nuggets

tuna fish sandwich

pepperoni pizza

Choose a snack:

fruit roll-up

yogurt

fresh fruit

Which one of these options is not a food group?

a. Vegetables and fruits

b. Dairy

c. Protein

d. Fats

e. Grains

Answer: Fats are not a food group. Limit solid fats, such as butter, fatty meats, or packaged snacks.

22

Learning more

Websites

Learn more about the MyPlate healthy eating guide at:

www.choosemyplate.gov/kids

Discover fun games, activities, and more at:

www.aboutkidshealth.ca/En/JustForKids/Life/Nutrition/Pages/nutrition.aspx

Get great recipe ideas, including ones for kids with health issues at:

kidshealth.org/kid/recipes

Books

Fulcher, Roz. *Be Good to Your Body: Healthy Eating and Fun Recipe*s. Dover, 2012.

Gleisner, Jenna Lee. *My Body Needs Food*. Amicus, 2014.

Knighton, Kate. *Why Shouldn't I Eat Junk Food?* Usborne, 2015.

Kreisman, Rachelle. *You Want Me to Eat That? A Kids' Guide to Eating Right*. Lerner, 2014.

Olson, Gillia M. *My Plate and You*. Capstone, 2012.

Most websites with addresses that end in ".org" or ".gov" have current information that you can trust.

Words to know

dairy [DARE-ee] noun A group of foods and drinks that are made from animal milk

energy [en-ER-gee] noun The body or mind's ability to do work

fiber [FIE-ber] noun A material found in grain foods that moves waste through the digestive system

gluten [GLOOT-en] noun A protein found in some flours

grains [GRANE] noun A group of foods made from the dried seeds of grass-like plants

habit [HAB-it] noun A way someone usually acts or thinks

mineral [MIN-e-rell] noun A natural, solid material

nutrient [NEW-tree-ent] noun An ingredient in food that a body needs to function

nutritious [NEW-trish-ush] adjective Describes a food or drink that provides nutrients

protein [PRO-teen] noun A group of plant and animal foods that contain nutrients the body needs to function

serving [SIR-ving] noun An amount of drink or food consumed at one time

vitamin [VITE-e-men] noun Small materials that are vital to a body

Index

A noun is a person, place, or thing.
An adjective tells us what something is like.